TOEFL®
Vocabulary Flashcards

Other Kaplan Books for English Learners

TOEFL iBT with CD-ROM

Inside the TOEFL iBT

TOEFL Paper-and-Pencil

TOEIC Exam, Second Edition

Learn English Through Classic Literature Series

The Short Stories and Essays of Mark Twain

American Tales of Horror and the Supernatural

TOEFL®
Vocabulary Flashcards

Compiled by Katherine Connor Martin

KAPLAN

Editorial Editor: Jennifer Farthing
Senior Editor: Ruth Baygell
Production Editor: Caitlin Ostrow
Production Artist: Renée Mitchell
Cover Designer: Carly Schnur

Published by Kaplan Publishing, a division of Kaplan, Inc.
888 Seventh Ave.
New York, NY 10106

Printed in the United States of America

October 2006
10 9 8 7 6 5 4 3 2 1

ISBN-13: 978-1-4195-4205-3
ISBN-10: 1-4195-4205-2

Kaplan Publishing books are available at special quantity discounts to use for sales promotions, employee premiums, or educational purposes. Please call our Special Sales Department to order or for more information at 800-621-9621, ext. 4444, e-mail kaplanpubsales@kaplan.com, or write to Kaplan Publishing, 30 South Wacker Drive, Suite 2500, Chicago, IL 60606-7481.

HOW TO USE THIS BOOK

The Test of English as a Foreign Language is a standardized test designed to measure your ability to understand and use English as it is used in a North American university setting. Recent changes to the TOEFL have shifted its focus from how much you know about English to how well you comprehend, speak, and write English.

Whether you are taking the TOEFL Internet-based Test or TOEFL Pencil-and-Paper Kaplan's *TOEFL Vocabulary Flashcards* is perfectly designed to help you learn 350 important TOEFL vocabulary words. Simply read the vocabulary word and its part of speech on the front of the flashcard to determine whether you know it; on the reverse, its definition and a sample sentence are offered to be sure that you understand the word's meaning and its correct, idiomatic usage.

These are followed by the corresponding noun, verb, adjective, or adverb forms. For each verb, the principal parts are given: *present participle, past tense,* and *past participle*. Thus you learn an average of four or more new words with each entry and augment your grasp of English grammar as well as your vocabulary. Once you've mastered a particular word, clip or fold back the corner of the flashcard so that you can zip by it to the words you still need to study.

The words are organized according to their part of speech: noun, verb, adjective, or adverb. You will notice, however, that they are not alphabetical. This is to help you focus on the individual word, its meaning, and its context. Words listed alphabetically are harder to distinguish and learn because they look and sound alike.

Study the words in any order and start on any page. Remember to flip the book over and study the other half.

Good luck!

LEARN THE MOST USEFUL WORDS

Academic English, like any other language, recycles a relatively small number of words over and over again. By learning those words, you enhance your reading and listening skills dramatically for a modest investment of your time and effort.

In selecting the words for this book, particular attention was given to advanced verbs and sophisticated adjectives because they tend to produce more impressive sentences, whether spoken or written.

On the TOEFL, only a few words will be tested as actual vocabulary. While it is impossible to predict exactly which words will be tested, having a broad and varied vocabulary is bound to improve your performance on the exam and in your academic career. The more complete your English vocabulary is the more easily you will comprehend what you hear or read and the richer your own writing and speaking will be. In fact, having a strong vocabulary can compensate for weaknesses in other skills. Your responses on the test will be scored not only on your control of syntax, but also on fluency and richness of vocabulary.

This book provides a powerful word arsenal. Building on the basic English vocabulary you have accumulated in your studies, it offers 350 of the words that tend to appear most frequently in academic speaking and writing—the words emphasized in the new, more challenging TOEFL exam, and most useful for those intending serious academic study.

DECODING THE MEANINGS OF WORDS

Common Roots, Prefixes, and Suffixes

Particularly in Academic English, recognizing common prefixes, suffixes, and roots (mostly from Greek and Latin) can be a useful tool in deciphering a word's meaning. If you begin by identifying a word's root and then determine if a prefix or suffix has been added, you will quickly multiply the number of new vocabulary words you assimilate. Consider how many new words you can form just by adding a different prefix to the root *-tain* (from the Latin tenere meaning *to hold*).

entertain	to amuse	maintain	to keep in an existing state
detain	to hold	retain	to hold back, keep
obtain	to acquire	attain	to reach, achieve
contain	to hold, enclose	sustain	to support, nourish
abstain	to refrain from, avoid	pertain	to belong, relate

Knowing roots of words expands your vocabulary in two ways. First, instead of learning one word at a time, you can learn whole groups of related words, and remembering one helps you remember others. Second, recognizing these familiar roots and affixes can often get you "close enough" to the meaning of an otherwise unfamiliar word.

Suffixes Indicating Parts of Speech

Many Academic English word endings are clues to a word's part of speech.

Words that end in these suffixes are almost always nouns:

-ance/-ence	*-cy*	*-ent*	*er/-or*	*-ism*
-ity	*-ment*	*-ness*	*-tion*	

Words that end in these suffixes are almost always verbs:

-ate	*-en*	*-esce*	*-ify/-fy*	*-ize*

Words that end in these suffixes are almost always adjectives:

-able/-ible	*-a/-ial/-ical*	*-an/-ian*	*-ant/-ent*	*-ful*
-ic	*-ile*	*-ish*	*-ive*	*-less*
-ous/-ose	*-y*			

Adverbs are commonly formed by adding *-ly* to the adjective.

Memorization Techniques

The following are a few vocabulary-building techniques that have worked for many others with practice and time. Remember, too, you are not alone; involving friends or native speakers will speed your progress. The important thing is to find out which methods work—and which do not work—for you.

Review vocabulary in short study sessions. 15 minutes of intense study each morning or evening is better than hours of study just prior to taking a test.

Work systematically. Look for common roots, prefixes, and suffixes, and for cognates of words in your own language to help you make intelligent choices.

Look for context clues. Vocabulary words do not occur in isolation and can often have more than one meaning. Look beyond the literal translation.

Consider color-coding. Use different colored highlighters for different parts of speech, or use color to denote positive or negative connotation or other word categories that you find helpful.

Say the words aloud as you flip through the book. Repetition reinforces the words and aids your retention.

Read voraciously. Brain studies have demonstrated that reading comprehension and vocabulary acquisition are closely related.

Tag stuff. Put labels or stickers on household items, classroom objects, and other objects in your environment to boost your long-term memory of many common nouns.

Tie each word to your own life to make it more memorable. After reading the sentence in this book that demonstrates the meaning and usage of a word, write your own sentence to personalize it.

Take 5. Take 5 words from the book that may be applicable to many contexts and plan to put them in your next writing or speaking assignment. Then move on to 5 more words.

Practice with a friend. Together you can make these words more than an academic study.

Combine vocabulary and grammar reviews. For example, if you are learning comparisons, create more unique answers by using some of your newer adjectives.

TRIGGER
verb

in this way; as a result of this

*He came in second in the race and **thereby** earned a spot on the national team.*

triggering, triggered, triggered
to cause (something) to happen, to set off

A skier on the west side of the mountain ***triggered*** *an avalanche of cascading snow.*

n. trigger

THEREBY

adverb

VOLUNTEER

verb

mostly, mainly, primarily

The book focuses ***chiefly*** *on social history.*

volunteering, volunteered, volunteered

to offer to do something, usually without being asked, pressured, or paid

*When their babysitter canceled at the last minute, I **volunteered** to take care of their son.*

n. volunteer *adj.* voluntary *adv.* voluntarily

CHIEFLY

adverb

PREDICT

verb

in the not too distant past, not long ago

*I have always been very healthy, but I **recently** started feeling sick.*

adj. recent

predicting, predicted, predicted
to know what will happen in the future, to foresee

*Gamblers try to **predict** which horse will win a race.*

n. prediction, predictability *adj.* predictable *adv.* predictably

RECENTLY

adverb

ACCOMPANY

verb

in the end, ultimately

He can only say a few words now, but ***eventually*** *he will be able to speak fluently.*

n. eventuality *adj.* eventual

accompanying, accompanied, accompanied
to go or come along with

The Secretary of State ***accompanied*** *the President on his trip.*

n. accompaniment

EVENTUALLY
adverb

RELAX

verb

by way of

We flew back from Los Angeles ***via*** *Chicago.*

relaxing, relaxed, relaxed
to become less tense, to slacken

A massage will help your muscles to relax.

n. relaxation *adj.* relaxing, relaxed

VIA
adverb

APPROVE

verb

as a result, therefore, consequently

Filtering the water in the aquarium will make it cleaner and ***hence*** *healthier for your fish.*

approving, approved, approved

1. to consent to, to allow, or to endorse; 2. to believe to be correct or good

*The treasurer has to **approve** all expenses.*

*His parents don't **approve** of his career choice.*

n. approval *adj.* approving *adv.* approvingly

HENCE

adverb

close to but not precisely, nearly, about

Approximately *5 percent of Americans commute to work using public transportation.*

v. approximate *n.* approximation *adj.* approximate, approximated

RESTRICT

verb

restricting, restricted, restricted
to limit, to reduce

*Laws **restrict** the amount of tobacco a person can bring into the country.*

n. restriction *adj.* restrictive *adv.* restrictively

APPROXIMATELY

adverb

VIOLATE

verb

similarly; in the same way; also

I couldn't afford to fly home, and a train ticket was ***likewise*** *beyond my means.*

violating, violated, violated
to defy, to disobey

By speaking to the press he ***violated*** *our contract.*

n. violation

LIKEWISE
adverb

DENY

verb

on the whole, in general

Sally's Pizza has great crust, but I think Pepe's pizza is better ***overall.***

denying, denied, denied

1. to dispute the truth of (a statement or fact); 2. to reject or refuse (a request)

*Her son **denied** that he had dented the car.*

*They **denied** our request for an extension.*

n. denial *adj.* deniable

OVERALL

adverb

IMMIGRATE

verb

in addition, additionally, moreover

She likes the biology program at that university, and ***furthermore***, *they offered her a scholarship.*

immigrating, immigrated, immigrated
to move to a new country

*Millions of Italians **immigrated** to the United States between 1880 and 1915.*

n. immigration, immigrant

FURTHERMORE

adverb

CONFORM

verb

in the beginning, to begin with, at the start

The cost of owning a car turned out to be much higher than we ***initially*** *expected.*

adj. initial

conforming, conformed, conformed

1. to follow rules or standards; 2. to follow social conventions, to fit in

Your new refrigerator should ***conform*** *to energy efficiency standards.*

Unlike his free-spirited, artistic sister, he has always tried to ***conform****.*

n. conformity, conformist *adj.* conformist

INITIALLY

adverb

ACKNOWLEDGE

verb

in spite of that, nonetheless

Educational opportunities for women were limited in the nineteenth century; ***nevertheless****, women contributed to that era's scientific accomplishments.*

acknowledging, acknowledged, acknowledged
to admit or accept as a fact, to recognize

*You should **acknowledge** that your mistakes caused the accident.*

n. acknowledgment *adj.* acknowledged

NEVERTHELESS

adverb

ASSEMBLE

verb

certainly, assuredly

*It is **definitely** going to be sunny tomorrow.*

adj. definite, definitive *adv.* definitively

assembling, assembled, assembled

1. to put (something) together; 2. to come together

*The engine was **assembled** from spare parts.*

*All students will **assemble** in the cafeteria this afternoon.*

n. assembly

DEFINITELY

adverb

EXPOSE

verb

following this, later, afterward, thereafter

She retired from her banking job at age 65 and ***subsequently*** *became involved in charity work.*

adj. subsequent

exposing, exposed, exposed

1. to reveal, to uncover; 2. to make vulnerable, to put in contact with something dangerous

*The journalist **exposed** a bribery scandal in the mayor's office.*

*The explosion in the factory **exposed** workers to dangerous chemicals.*

n. exposure, exposé *adj.* exposed

SUBSEQUENTLY

adverb

INTERPRET

verb

as a result, for this reason, therefore, accordingly

Regular exercise leads to better health and ***consequently*** *to a longer life.*

n. consequence *adj.* consequent

interpreting, interpreted, interpreted

to explain or understand the meaning of, to translate

He says that he can ***interpret*** *people's dreams.*

n. interpretation, interpreter *adj.* interpretive

CONSEQUENTLY

adverb

DEMONSTRATE

verb

a procedure for dealing with or approach to a public issue

The administration is developing a new ***policy*** *on immigration.*

demonstrating, demonstrated, demonstrated
to show, to prove, or to establish (a principle, theory, etc.) with evidence

*Research has **demonstrated** that this new medication is five times as effective.*

n. demonstration, demonstrator *adj.* demonstrable, demonstrative *adv.* demonstrably, demonstratively

POLICY
noun

ADJUST
verb

an idea that forms the foundation of a theory or of a system of morality
The ***principle*** *of equality is an important part of true democracy.*
adj: principled

adjusting, adjusted, adjusted
to change or alter (something) slightly in order to improve it, to modify

*You may need to **adjust** your television antenna for better reception.*

n. adjustment *adj.* adjusted

PRINCIPLE

noun

DIMINISH

verb

a subject for study or discussion

*The **topic** of her paper is animal life in rainforests.*

adj. topical *adv.* topically

diminishing, diminished, diminished
to become less or worse, to decline

His influence in the company ***diminished*** *after his successor was chosen.*

adj. diminished, diminishing

TOPIC

noun

ACQUIRE

verb

something that is not like others of its type; an anomaly

Most mammals give birth to live young; the platypus, which lays eggs, is an ***exception.***

adj. exceptional *adv.* exceptionally

acquiring, acquired, acquired
to obtain or receive, to attain

*During his year in Berlin he **acquired** a perfect German accent.*

n. acquisition

EXCEPTION

noun

INFLUENCE

verb

order

The numbers in the code have to be entered in the right ***sequence****.*

v. sequence *adj.* sequential, sequenced *adv.* sequentially

influencing, influenced, influenced
to have an effect on, to affect, to impact

*Current events **influenced** his recent writing.*

n. influence *adj.* influential, influenced

SEQUENCE

noun

a large area that is considered to have unifying characteristics

*The southwestern **region** of the United States is known for its desert climate.*

adj. regional *adv.* regionally

REVISE

verb

revising, revised, revised

1. to reconsider; 2. to improve (a piece of writing, etc.) by changing it

*Upon this discovery, astronomers **revised** their definition of a planet.*

*My teacher told me that if I **revise** the essay I will get a better grade.*

n. revision, revisionism *adj.* revised, revisionary, revisionist

REGION

noun

ABSORB

verb

a single person

Identical twins often complain that people tend to treat them as a pair, rather than as ***individuals.***

n. individuality, individualism, individualist *adj.* individual, individualistic, individualized *adv.* individually

absorbing, absorbed, absorbed
to take in or soak up

*A sponge can **absorb** a lot of liquid.*

n. absorption *adj.* absorbed, absorbing

INDIVIDUAL
noun

PURCHASE

verb

1. a difficult task or undertaking; 2. a questioning of authority

*The marathon is a **challenge** even for experienced runners.*

*Impressionist paintings were seen as a **challenge** to traditional artistic standards.*

v. challenge *n.* challenger *adj.* challenging, challenged

purchasing, purchased, purchased

to buy

*They are raising money to **purchase** new computers for the school.*

n. purchase, purchaser

CHALLENGE

noun

SELECT

verb

an impression, an effect

*The film had a great **impact** on me; I was really moved.*

v. impact *adj.* impacted

selecting, selected, selected
to choose

*The judges **selected** five dancers as finalists.*

n. selection, selector *adj.* selective, select *adv.* selectively

IMPACT

noun

INTERVENE

verb

intensive study of a particular topic

She is doing ***research*** *on local history.*

v. research *n.* researcher

intervening, intervened, intervened
to become involved in a situation, to interfere

A fight broke out during the school dance, but the chaperones ***intervened*** *before anyone was hurt.*

n. intervention *adj.* intervening

RESEARCH

noun

ENHANCE

verb

weather conditions over a long period of time; the environment

Scientists are studying the forces causing changes in the ***climate.***

adj. climatic

enhancing, enhanced, enhanced
to make better, to improve

*Dressing neatly for a job interview will **enhance** your likelihood of getting hired.*

n. enhancement *adj.* enhanced

CLIMATE

noun

MOTIVATE

verb

the way something looks

It is a beautiful old house, but the broken windows ruin its ***appearance.***

v. appear *adj.* apparent *adv.* apparently

motivating, motivated, motivated
to give (a person) a reason or incentive to do something, to encourage or inspire

*Our coach **motivates** us to practice harder by setting goals.*

n. motive, motivation *adj.* motivated

APPEARANCE

noun

IMPLY

verb

income; money that is earned

The store has had much higher ***revenues*** *this year.*

implying, implied, implied

to suggest that something is true without saying so directly, to insinuate

*Although he didn't complain, his reaction **implied** that he was disappointed.*

n. implication *adj.* implicit, implied

REVENUE

noun

REVEAL

verb

a system of ideas that is meant to explain a complex phenomenon; a belief, thesis, or hypothesis

Scientists are developing new ***theories*** *about the nature of the universe.*

v. theorize *n.* theorist *adj.* theoretical *adv.* theoretically

revealing, revealed, revealed
to show, to uncover

*The curtains were pulled back to **reveal** a beautiful view.*

n. revelation *adj.* revealing

THEORY

noun

IMPLEMENT

verb

1. the way in which the parts of something are put together; organization; 2. a building or construction

The ***structure*** *of a typical essay involves an introduction at the beginning and a conclusion at the end.*

The ruins include a large, low ***structure*** *that might have been used to store grain.*

v. structure *adj.* structural, structured *adv.* structurally

implementing, implemented, implemented

to put into effect, to enact

*We will be **implementing** a new grading system next semester.*

n. implement, implementation

STRUCTURE

noun

THRIVE

verb

a short description of the content of a longer piece of writing, film, etc.

*We were asked to write a one-page **summary** of the book.*

v. summarize *n.* summarization *adj.* summarized

thriving, thrived/throve, thrived/thriven
to flourish, to do well, to prosper

*This plant will **thrive** in a warm, wet climate.*

SUMMARY

noun

STRIVE

verb

something considered to be of the highest importance

We will eventually paint the house, but right now our ***priority*** *is to finish the roof.*

v. prioritize *n.* prioritization

striving, strove/strived, striven/strived

to try, to attempt or endeavor

*She **strove** to be a role model for female athletes.*

n. striver

PRIORITY

noun

REQUIRE
verb

a belief that is not based on proof

Historians must be careful not to make ***assumptions*** *about the past based on today's values.*

v. assume *adj.* assumed

requiring, required, required
to need or demand

*Finishing a crossword puzzle **requires** a lot of patience.*

n. requirement *adj.* required

ASSUMPTION
noun

ACCELERATE

verb

money that is paid to a person or company; salary; earnings

If she gets promoted, her ***income*** *will increase substantially.*

accelerating, accelerated, accelerated
to gain speed, to speed up

*The gas pedal makes a car **accelerate**.*

n. acceleration

INCOME

noun

a fixed order of things by status or importance

*There was a strict **hierarchy** in medieval European society, with the king at the top and the peasants on the bottom.*

adj. hierarchical *adv.* hierarchically

RESPOND

verb

responding, responded, responded
to answer; to reply

Only half of the people we contacted ***responded*** *to our survey.*

n. response, respondent, responsiveness *adj.* responsive

HIERARCHY

noun

REJECT

verb

all of the people who are born within a particular period of time

*The **generation** of Americans born right after World War II are often called the "baby boomers."*

rejecting, rejected, rejected

to refuse to accept, to dismiss

*Very few scientists entirely **reject** this theory.*

n. reject, rejection *adj.* rejected

GENERATION

noun

DERIVE

verb

the power or right to make decisions or judgments about something

Only Congress has the ***authority*** *to officially declare war.*

adj. authoritative *adv.* authoritatively

deriving, derived, derived
to obtain (something) from a source

All of the ingredients in this shampoo are ***derived*** *from plants.*

n. derivation, derivative *adj.* derived, derivative

AUTHORITY

noun

INVEST
verb

a long period in history that has defining characteristics

*She recommended a book about the colonial **era.***

investing, invested, invested

to put money into (stocks, a business, real estate, etc.) in the hope of making a profit

*He made his fortune by **investing** in the stock market.*

n. investment, investor

ERA

noun

something that is aimed for; a goal

To meet our ***target,*** *we have to increase sales by 15 percent.*

v. target *adj.* targeted

INVESTIGATE

verb

investigating, investigated, investigated

to look closely at (something) in order to determine the truth, to examine

The police are ***investigating*** *his connections to organized crime.*

v. investigation, investigator *adj.* investigative

TARGET

noun

DECLINE

verb

a government, usually one that is oppressive and authoritarian

Her book discusses the various groups that opposed the Nazi ***regime.***

declining, declined, declined

1. to become lower or worse, to decrease or diminish; 2. to choose not to do something, to refuse

*The price of gold has **declined** since last year.*

*I **declined** their invitation to dinner.*

n. decline *adj.* declining

REGIME

noun

UTILIZE

verb

a practice or belief that has existed for a long time; a custom

Our family has a ***tradition*** *of eating fish for dinner on Christmas Eve.*

n. traditionalist *adj.* traditional *adv.* traditionally

utilizing, utilized, utilized

to use

*Our system **utilizes** the most advanced technology.*

n. utilization, utility

TRADITION

noun

SEEK

verb

a plan for how to do something; a method

In chess, it is important to have a strong ***strategy*** *from the beginning of the game.*

v. strategize *n.* strategist *adj.* strategic *adv.* strategically

seeking, sought, sought
to look for

*They are **seeking** applicants for a paralegal job.*

n. seeker

STRATEGY

noun

ENCOUNTER

verb

a condition or fact that affects an event or creates a situation

The room was cold and dark, and she hadn't slept the night before; it is difficult to take a test under those ***circumstances****.*

adj. circumstantial

encountering, encountered, encountered
to meet; to face

*The plans for a new shopping mall **encountered** opposition in the city council.*

n. encounter

CIRCUMSTANCE

noun

INVOLVE

verb

plural: *hypotheses*

an unproven theory, especially a scientific one

*Her **hypothesis** was that the mice eating the special diet would grow twice as fast.*

v. hypothesize *adj.* hypothetical *adv.* hypothetically

involving, involved, involved
to make (someone) a part of something

*I don't want to get **involved** with this; it sounds like a terrible idea.*

n. involvement *adj.* involved

HYPOTHESIS

noun

ANTICIPATE

verb

plural: *analyses*

a detailed interpretation of information

An ***analysis*** *of the test results showed gradual improvement in math scores.*

n. analyst *v.* analyze *adj.* analytical, analyzed *adv.* analytically

anticipating, anticipated, anticipated
to expect or look forward to

Experts ***anticipate*** *a major victory by the opposition party in this election.*

n. anticipation *adj.* anticipated, anticipatory

ANALYSIS

noun

MODIFY

verb

plural: *emphases*

special attention, stress, prominence

The new laws put ***emphasis*** *on protecting the environment.*

v. emphasize *adj.* emphatic *adv.* emphatically

modifying, modified, modified
to adapt; to change or adjust

*She **modified** her car to run on solar power as well as gasoline.*

n. modification *adj.* modified

EMPHASIS

noun

UNDERGO

verb

a speech intended to teach something

Are you going to Professor Smith's ***lecture*** *on the Cold War?*

v. lecture *n.* lecturer

undergoing, underwent, undergone
to experience, to be subjected to

*The website **underwent** a complete remodeling.*

LECTURE

noun

UNDERLIE

verb

a remark that expresses an observation or opinion

We never had a chance to give our ***comments*** *on the proposal.*

v. comment *n.* commentary, commentator

underlying, underlay, underlain

1. to be located beneath; 2. to be a cause or reason for something

The layer of rock that ***underlies*** *the earth's crust is called the mantle.*

Numerous issues ***underlie*** *the failure of the peace talks.*

adj. underlying

COMMENT

noun

UNDERTAKE

verb

what something is used for; purpose or utility

Archaeologists are uncertain about the ***function*** *of these ancient stone tools.*

v. function *n.* functionality *adj.* functional, functioning *adv.* functionally

undertaking, undertook, undertaken
to attempt, to take on (a task or job); to tackle

*They are **undertaking** a survey of the surrounding land.*

n. undertaking

FUNCTION

noun

a dominant pattern or direction; a tendency

*The **trend** towards larger and larger vehicles has begun to change.*

TRANSLATE

verb

translating, translated, translated
to interpret, to express in another language

*He is **translating** the plays of Shakespeare into Spanish.*

n. translation, translator

TREND

noun

TERMINATE

verb

a piece of writing

The class will discuss **texts** *by six major twentieth-century thinkers.*

adj. textual

terminating, terminated, terminated
to end, to bring or come to a close

*The landlord **terminated** our rental agreement, so we have to move.*

n. termination

TEXT

noun

PROHIBIT
verb

a point of view

I'd like to hear your ***perspective*** on this issue.

prohibiting, prohibited, prohibited
to forbid or ban

*Smoking is **prohibited** in this building.*

n. prohibition *adj.* prohibitive, prohibited

PERSPECTIVE

noun

PARTICIPATE

verb

a style or category, especially a type of literature, etc.

*He prefers books in the **genre** of science fiction.*

participating, participated, participated

to take part in, to be involved in

All students are required to ***participate*** *in after-school activities.*

n. participation, participant *adj.* participatory, participating

GENRE

noun

DISCRIMINATE

verb

a period of ten years

The Great Depression of the 1930s lasted an entire ***decade****.*

discriminating, discriminated, discriminated

1. to treat differently because of prejudice; 2. to detect differences, especially small or subtle ones, to differentiate or distinguish

*Universities once **discriminated** against women and minorities in their admissions practices.*

*Newborn babies can't **discriminate** between different colors.*

n. discrimination *adj.* discriminatory, discriminating

DECADE

noun

COMPRISE

verb

an attitude that is unfairly positive or negative about a particular group, person, or thing in comparison to others; prejudice

The company is accused of ***bias*** *against the elderly in its hiring practices.*

adj. biased

comprising, comprised, comprised
to be made up of, to consist of, to incorporate

*The United States of America **comprises** 50 individual states.*

BIAS

noun

CONSIST

verb

work, especially physical work

Without a ride-on mower, mowing your lawn can be exhausting ***labor.***

v. labor *adj.* laborious *adv.* laboriously

consisting, consisted, consisted

to be made up (of)

*A single deck **consists** of 52 playing cards—13 of each suit.*

LABOR

noun

VARY

verb

a person who has special knowledge or experience in a particular field

The museum called in an ***expert*** *to determine if the painting was a forgery.*

n. expertise *adj.* expert *adv.* expertly

varying, varied, varied
to change

*The town's population **varies** with the season, as the tourists come and go.*

n. variation, variant, variance, variety *adj.* various, variable, varied *adv.* variously, variably

EXPERT

noun

RELY

verb

the length of time that something lasts

Please remain seated for the ***duration*** *of the flight.*

relying, relied, relied
to be dependent (on something)

*I **rely** on the financial aid money to pay for school.*

n. reliance, reliability *adj.* reliant, reliable *adv.* reliably

DURATION

noun

an image, etc., that represents something else; a sign
The raven in the poem is often interpreted as a ***symbol*** *of death.*
v. symbolize *n.* symbolism *adj.* symbolic *adv.* symbolically

SUBSTITUTE
verb

substituting, substituted, substituted
to replace

The recipe works just as well if you ***substitute*** *oranges for lemons.*

n. substitute, substitution

SYMBOL

noun

a plan or technique for achieving a goal, a strategy

The new ***tactics*** *introduced by our coach helped us win the game.*

n. tactician *adj.* tactical *adv.* tactically

EVALUATE

verb

evaluating, evaluated, evaluated
to assess, judge, or estimate

*An engineer **evaluated** the condition of the house.*

n. evaluation

TACTIC

noun

OUTGROW

verb

a story, an account of connected events

*The Odyssey is a long **narrative** in the form of a poem.*

v. narrate *n.* narration *adj.* narrative *adv.* narratively

outgrowing, outgrew, outgrown

to no longer need or be able to use (something) due to growth or development

*She used to love this dress but she has **outgrown** it.*

NARRATIVE

noun

singular: *medium*

the news and entertainment outlets such as the press, television, radio, and film

The politician was unhappy with the way he had been depicted in the ***media.***

APPRECIATE

verb

appreciating, appreciated, appreciated
to be grateful for

*I really **appreciate** your generous help.*

n. appreciation *adj.* appreciative, appreciable *adv.* appreciatively, appreciably

MEDIA
noun

MONITOR

verb

singular: *datum*

information

The report is based on ***data*** *collected over 25 years.*

monitoring, monitored, monitored
to observe, to keep track of

After I got into debt, my parents started ***monitoring*** *my spending.*

n. monitor *adj.* monitored

DATA

noun

CONSTRUCT

verb

natural skill or ability

He has an amazing ***talent*** *for music.*

adj. talented

constructing, constructed, constructed
to build or form

The first rule of essay writing is to ***construct*** *a convincing argument.*

n. construction, construct *adj.* constructive, constructed

TALENT

noun

ESTABLISH

verb

1. a small part of a whole, less than half; 2. a member of a group that accounts for less than half of a population

*Atheists are a **minority** in the United States.*

*The company is recruiting **minorities** for positions on its board of directors.*

establishing, established, established

1. to set up (an institution, etc.), to found; 2. to show that something is a fact

Yellowstone Park was ***established*** *in 1872.*

The prosecutor can ***establish*** *that the defendant was there at the time of the robbery.*

n. establishment *adj.* established

MINORITY

noun

CONCLUDE
verb

the largest part of a whole, over half

*The **majority** of Americans prefer coffee to tea.*

concluding, concluded, concluded

1. to finish, to end; 2. to develop a judgment after studying or considering something

*The play **concludes** with a joyful wedding scene.*

*By the end of the meeting, we had **concluded** that your plan was best.*

n. conclusion *adj.* conclusive, concluded, concluding *adv.* conclusively

MAJORITY

noun

SURVIVE
verb

any of multiple options, another possibility

Whole grains such as barley are exciting and healthy ***alternatives*** *to pasta.*

adj. alternative *adv.* alternatively

surviving, survived, survived
to last or live through an event or period of time, to endure

Only a few books ***survived*** *the fire in the library.*

n. survival, survivor *adj.* surviving

ALTERNATIVE

noun

RECOMMEND

verb

a chance to do something

The recital will give her an ***opportunity*** *to demonstrate her talent.*

adj. opportune *adv.* opportunely

recommending, recommended, recommended

1. to advise; 2. to say positive things about, to endorse

*The doctor **recommended** that I avoid salty foods.*

*My friend **recommends** this movie.*

n. recommendation *adj.* recommended

OPPORTUNITY

noun

evidence showing that a statement or fact is true, verification

New customers are required to show ***proof*** *that they live in the neighborhood.*

SCRUTINIZE
verb

scrutinizing, scrutinized, scrutinized
to closely inspect or examine

The results were unexpected, but after ***scrutinizing*** *the data we determined it was accurate.*

n. scrutiny

PROOF
noun

POLLUTE

verb

a stock of information, skill, money, etc., that can be used to make or accomplish something

Do you have enough ***resources*** *to carry out this project?*

adj. resourceful

polluting, polluted, polluted
to contaminate or make unclean

*The river has been **polluted** by chemicals from the factory.*

n. pollution, pollutant *adj.* polluted

RESOURCE

noun

SIMULATE

verb

flexibility, freedom, room for variation or to maneuver

The camp counselors were given a lot of ***leeway*** *in how they chose to enforce the rules.*

simulating, simulated, simulated
to imitate; to mimic

*Astronauts train in water to **simulate** the experience of weightlessness.*

n. simulation, simulator *adj.* simulated

LEEWAY

noun

ENSURE

verb

1. variety, especially in terms of culture or ethnicity; 2. multiformity

*The **diversity** of the student body has increased significantly in the past decade.*

*Scientists fear that climate change will lead to less **diversity** of animal and plant species.*

v. diversify *n.* diversification *adj.* diverse, diversified *adv.* diversely

ensuring, ensured, ensured

to make (something) certain; to guarantee

Snow tires should be used in the winter to ***ensure*** *safety on slippery roads.*

DIVERSITY

noun

an idea, especially one that is abstract and general

As an introduction, she explained the major ***concepts*** *that would be covered in the class.*

v. conceptualize *n.* conception, conceptualization *adj.* conceptual, conceptualized *adv.* conceptually

COMMENCE

verb

commencing, commenced, commenced
to begin

*Construction of the new chemistry building will **commence** next week.*

n. commencement

CONCEPT

noun

APPROACH
verb

the sex (male or female) of a person
*Discrimination based on **gender** is illegal.*
adj. gendered

approaching, approached, approached
to come close to

*Temperatures **approached** record highs last summer.*

n. approach *adj.* approachable

GENDER

noun

CONSULT

verb

an example of an action or phenomenon; an occurrence; an occasion

It was just one more ***instance*** *of personal failure.*

consulting, consulted, consulted
to seek advice or information from

*You should **consult** your lawyer before signing a contract.*

n. consultation, consultancy, consultant, consulting *adj.* consultative

INSTANCE

noun

DISTRACT

verb

ability, skill, competence

Before studying abroad, students are expected to achieve basic ***proficiency*** *in a foreign language.*

adj. proficient *adv.* proficiently

distracting, distracted, distracted
to divert or take away someone's attention

The music is ***distracting*** *me from my work.*

n. distraction *adj.* distracting

PROFICIENCY

noun

ENABLE

verb

---

a result

*The **outcome** of the election was a surprise to everyone.*

enabling, enabled, enabled
to make able or possible

*A new computer would **enable** us to work faster.*

n. enabler

OUTCOME

noun

ASSESS

verb

a reward for doing something

To attract new members, the gym is offering ***incentives*** *such as free yoga classes.*

assessing, assessed, assessed
To judge the nature, quality, or degree of (something), to evaluate or appraise

Students were asked to ***assess*** *the accuracy of information they found on the Internet.*

n. assessment, assessor *adj.* assessable, assessed

INCENTIVE

noun

PERSIST

verb

intense public disagreement about something, a debate

*A **controversy** arose over the school's new science curriculum.*

adj. controversial *adv.* controversially

persisting, persisted, persisted
to last, to go on, to endure

*The bad weather is expected to **persist** for another week.*

n. persistence *adj.* persistent *adv.* persistently

CONTROVERSY

noun

DEVOTE

verb

a position or site, a place

They still haven't found a good ***location*** *for their new restaurant.*

v. locate *adj.* located

devoting, devoted, devoted
to commit, to dedicate

Gandhi ***devoted*** *his life to opposing discrimination and oppression.*

n. devotion, devotee *adj.* devoted *adv.* devotedly

LOCATION
noun

CEASE

verb

a strong and rigid system of belief; dogma

The Communist ***ideology*** *was very influential during the twentieth century.*

n. ideologue *adj.* ideological *adv.* ideologically

ceasing, ceased, ceased
to end, to conclude, to stop

*A treaty was signed last night, and the fighting finally **ceased**.*

n. cessation *adj.* ceaseless

IDEOLOGY

noun

DOUBT

verb

importance in relation to others, rank

People often judge the social ***status*** *of others based on the way they dress.*

doubting, doubted, doubted
to suspect of being untrue

*The police have begun to **doubt** his version of events.*

n. doubt *adj.* doubtful *adv.* doubtfully

STATUS
noun

PRECEDE

verb

a person seeking a position, especially a person running for election to public office

She is one of three ***candidates*** *for governor.*

preceding, preceded, preceded
to go or come before

Twenty policemen on motorcycles ***preceded*** *the president's limousine.*

n. precedent, precedence *adj.* preceding

CANDIDATE

noun

UNIFY
verb

knowledge and good judgment based on experience; good sense

The decision demonstrated her ***wisdom.***

adj. wise *adv.* wisely

unifying, unified, unified
to bring or come together, to unite

*East and West Germany were **unified** in 1990.*

n. unification, unifier *adj.* unified, unifying

WISDOM

noun

INSERT

verb

a stage

Before becoming a butterfly, a caterpillar goes through a "chrysalis" ***phase.***

inserting, inserted, inserted

to put (something) into something else

*To start the program, **insert** the disk and follow the instructions.*

n. insertion

PHASE

noun

DETERIORATE

verb

something that must be done beforehand, a requirement or precondition

Introductory English 101 is a ***prerequisite*** *for the advanced creative writing course.*

adj. prerequisite

deteriorating, deteriorated, deteriorated
to grow worse

*The patient's condition has **deteriorated** since last night.*

n. deterioration *adj.* deteriorating

PREREQUISITE

noun

CORRESPONDING

verb

the way that a person acts, conduct

They criticized his ***behavior*** *during the game.*

v. behave *adj.* behavioral *adv.* behaviorally

corresponding, corresponded, corresponded

1. to be very similar to something, to match almost exactly; 2. to exchange letters

The Greek letter alpha ***corresponds*** *with the letter "A" in the Roman alphabet.*

I have ***corresponded*** *with her for several months.*

n. correspondence, correspondent *adj.* corresponding

BEHAVIOR noun

1. the field of banking and investments; 2. (in plural) a person's or company's situation with respect to money

*My brother is a stockbroker, and I also plan to have a career in **finance**.*

*My **finances** are very bad right now, and I am afraid the bank will reject my loan application.*

v. finance *n.* financier, financing *adj.* financial *adv.* financially

COOPERATE

verb

cooperating, cooperated, cooperated

to work together in order to accomplish something, to collaborate

The United States and Canada ***cooperated*** *to fight smuggling over their shared border.*

n. cooperation *adj.* cooperative *adv.* cooperatively

FINANCE

noun

DOMINATE

verb

a new way of doing something, an invention

*The VCR was a major **innovation** in the way people watched films.*

v. innovate *n.* innovator *adj.* innovative *adv.* innovatively

dominating, dominated, dominated
to exert control over

*Our basketball team **dominated** the game.*

n. domination, dominance *adj.* dominant

INNOVATION

noun

FACILITATE

verb

one who shares an activity, business, etc.

She's looking for a new tennis ***partner.***

n. partnership

facilitating, facilitated, facilitated

to make (something) easier

*Railroads **facilitated** the settlement of the midwestern United States.*

n. facilitator, facilitation

PARTNER

noun

RETAIN
verb

a state or incident of disagreement or hostility, a clash

There is often a ***conflict*** *between one's personal desires and the best interest of society.*

v. conflict *adj.* conflicting, conflicted

retaining, retained, retained
to keep or hold

*The town **retains** much of its historic charm.*

n. retention, retainer *adj.* retentive

CONFLICT

noun

COMPLEMENT

verb

1. the group of people responsible for managing a company, government, etc.; management; 2. the act of administering

The proposal has to be approved by the University ***administration.***

She is going to business school to get a degree in ***administration.***

v. administer, administrate *n.* administrator *adj.* administrative *adv.* administratively

complementing, complemented, complemented

to bring out the best in or supply a missing quality to, to be the ideal partner or accompaniment

*The rich flavor of the wine **complemented** the steak perfectly.*

n. complement *adj.* complementary

ADMINISTRATION

noun

COMPLIMENT

verb

economic activity, trade, business

The new policies are supposed to encourage ***commerce*** *by helping small businesses.*

adj. commercial *adv.* commercially

complimenting, complimented, complimented
to make a positive comment about, to praise

*He **complimented** her excellent taste in music.*

n. compliment *adj.* complimentary

COMMERCE

noun

1. a circular movement, a rotation or turn; 2. a dramatic change, especially the overthrow of a government

Earth completes a ***revolution*** *around the sun every 365¼ days.*

The American ***Revolution*** *overthrew an English colonial government; the French* ***Revolution*** *unseated a native ruling class.*

v. revolve, revolutionize *n.* revolutionary, revolt *adj.* revolutionary

OCCUPY

verb

occupying, occupied, occupied

1. to be in (a place or position), to inhabit; 2. to engage, employ, or keep busy

*They **occupied** the house for months without paying rent.*

*The toy **occupied** the boy for hours.*

n. occupancy, occupant, occupier, occupation *adj.* occupied

REVOLUTION

noun

MANIPULATE

verb

a way of doing something, a technique

They are developing a new ***method*** *for learning to read music.*

n. methodology *adj.* methodical, methodological *adv.* methodically; methodologically

manipulating, manipulated, manipulated
to influence or control

*He **manipulated** his grandmother into leaving him money in her will.*

n. manipulation, manipulator *adj.* manipulative, manipulated *adv.* manipulatively

METHOD

noun

WAIVE

verb

a mistake

This report contains an unacceptable number of ***errors.***

v. err *adj.* erroneous *adv.* erroneously

waiving, waived, waived
to give up, to relinquish

*She **waived** her right to a lawyer.*

n. waiver

ERROR

noun

CONVINCE
verb

1. the act of publishing a text; 2. a published book, journal, magazine, etc.

He is excited about the ***publication*** *of his first novel.*

She has written articles for several different ***publications.***

convincing, convinced, convinced
to cause (a person) to agree with a statement or opinion, to persuade

*I finally **convinced** him that I was right.*

adj. convincing, convinced *adv.* convincingly

PUBLICATION

noun

PERCEIVE
verb

information derived from numerical analysis

The latest ***statistics*** *show an increase in the rate of population growth.*

n. statistician *adj.* statistical *adv.* statistically

perceiving, perceived, perceived
to sense, to be aware of

*Dogs **perceive** a greater range of sounds than humans can.*

n. perception *adj.* perceived, perceptible *adv.* perceptibly

STATISTIC

noun

ATTRIBUTE
verb

reason; rational thinking
The problem has to be solved with ***logic.***
n. logician *adj.* logical *adv.* logically

attributing, attributed, attributed

to give credit or assign responsibility for (something) to a particular person, condition, etc.

*He **attributes** his good health to a low-fat diet and plenty of exercise.*

n. attribution *adj.* attributable, attributed

LOGIC

noun

OCCUR

verb

understanding or appreciation

This book gave me greater ***insight*** *into modern politics.*

adj. insightful *adv.* insightfully

occurring, occurred, occurred
to happen, to take place

*The burglary **occurred** late last night.*

n. occurrence

INSIGHT

noun

INTIMIDATE

verb

a choice or possibility

There are several different ***options*** *for getting Internet access.*

adj. optional *adv.* optionally

intimidating, intimidated, intimidated

to challenge (a person's) confidence; to make nervous or afraid

*His students' knowledge sometimes **intimidates** him.*

n. intimidation *adj.* intimidating

OPTION

noun

REINFORCE

verb

facts that support a theory or assertion

Although many believed she was guilty, there wasn't enough ***evidence*** *to prosecute her for the crime.*

adj. evident, evidential, evidenced *adv.* evidently

reinforcing, reinforced, reinforced
to make stronger or more intense

He is very close-minded; he only reads books that ***reinforce*** *his own beliefs.*

n. reinforcement *adj.* reinforced

EVIDENCE
noun

PURSUE
verb

the base that something is built on; basis; underpinning
Charles Darwin's theory of natural selection is the ***foundation*** *of modern biology.*
adj. foundational

pursuing, pursued, pursued
to follow or chase after

*The dogs **pursued** the fox through the field.*

n. pursuit, pursuer

FOUNDATION

noun

plural: *phenomena*

something that exists or occurs, especially something remarkable, an occurrence, a wonder

The annual migration of the monarch butterflies is an incredible natural ***phenomenon.***

adj. phenomenal *adv.* phenomenally

CONCENTRATE

verb

concentrating, concentrated, concentrated
to focus, to direct one's attention to

*My teacher suggested that I **concentrate** on improving my writing.*

n. concentration

PHENOMENON

noun

IGNORE

verb

a general survey

*This book offers an **overview** of the major developments in astronomy since the time of Galileo.*

ignoring, ignored, ignored
to pay no attention to

*Whenever my little brother annoyed me, my mother just told me to **ignore** him.*

adj. ignored

OVERVIEW

noun

DETECT

verb

ability or promise

*Her coach thinks she has the **potential** to be a world-class athlete.*

adv. potentially

detecting, detected, detected

to sense or discover something, to discern, to identify

*I **detected** some uncertainty in her voice as she answered.*

n. detection, detective, detector *adj.* detectable *adv.* detectably

POTENTIAL

noun

EXPAND

verb

situated between two stages, in the middle

*Before moving on to the advanced class, I am going to try the **intermediate** level.*

expanding, expanded, expanded

to move apart or outwards so as to take up more space, to grow

*In the 1920s, scientists discovered that the universe is **expanding**.*

n. expansion, expansionism *adj.* expansive, expanding

INTERMEDIATE

adjective

CLARIFY

verb

extremely important, indispensable

The helicopter is delivering ***crucial*** *supplies to a remote hospital.*

n. crux *adv.* crucially

clarifying, clarified, clarified
to make something clearer or easier to understand, to explain

*The candidate had to **clarify** his statements about environmental policy.*

n. clarification, clarity *adj.* clarified

CRUCIAL
adjective

COMPARE

verb

difficult to understand, complicated

The problem was too ***complex*** *to be solved in a single meeting.*

n. complexity

comparing, compared, compared
to make note of differences and similarities between (two things)

*They **compared** the two cars to see which was the better deal.*

n. comparison *adj.* comparable *adv.* comparably

COMPLEX
adjective

REACT

verb

1. existing or happening at the same time; contemporaneous; 2. existing or happening in the present, modern

His childhood was ***contemporary*** *with the First World War.*

Their house is filled with fashionable ***contemporary*** *furniture.*

n. contemporary

reacting, reacted, reacted

to act in response to, to respond

*How did your mother **react** when you told her you were getting married?*

n. reaction *adj.* reactionary, reactive

CONTEMPORARY

adjective

CONVEY

verb

deeply rooted, essential, inherent

*Freedom of expression is an **intrinsic** American value.*

adv. intrinsically

conveying, conveyed, conveyed

1. to communicate or express; 2. to transport

She tried to ***convey*** *the seriousness of the situation, but they didn't seem to grasp it.*

The boxes were ***conveyed*** *to Boston by train.*

n. conveyance

INTRINSIC

adjective

COMBINE

verb

misleading, giving a false impression

The pictures were ***deceptive****—the apartment was actually quite small.*

v. deceive *n.* deception *adv.* deceptively

combining, combined, combined
to put together; to blend

Text messaging ***combines*** *the convenience of e-mail with the speed of a phone call.*

n. combination *adj.* combined

DECEPTIVE

adjective

DISTRIBUTE

verb

required, obligatory, compulsory

*Before the start of classes, new students must attend a **mandatory** orientation.*

distributing, distributed, distributed
to give out, to divide among a group

*We **distributed** the money evenly among the group.*

n. distribution, distributor *adj.* distributional

MANDATORY

adjective

PROMOTE

verb

of moderate quality or ability, unexceptional, passable

*She's an excellent guitarist but only **mediocre** as a drummer.*

n. mediocrity

promoting, promoted, promoted

1. to support or publicize; 2. to raise (someone) to a higher grade or position

Actors often go on television talk shows to ***promote*** *their new movies.*

Jay worked very hard at school, hoping he would be ***promoted****.*

n. promotion, promoter

MEDIOCRE

adjective

CONSUME

verb

relating to or affecting the entire world, widespread

*After years of operating locally, we have decided to become a **global** company serving people in many countries.*

n. globe, globalization *adv.* globally

consuming, consumed, consumed

1. to buy or use up; 2. to eat or drink

*Americans **consume** 25 percent of the world's oil.*

*He **consumed** the entire pie in under ten minutes.*

n. consumer, consumption *adj.* consuming

GLOBAL

adjective

DISTORT

verb

proper or suitable

Some parents worry that these video games may not be ***appropriate*** *for children.*

n. appropriateness *adv.* appropriately

distorting, distorted, distorted
to depict something inaccurately

That mirror ***distorts*** *your image so that you look taller than you are.*

n. distortion *adj.* distorted

APPROPRIATE

adjective

ELIMINATE

verb

belonging to neither of two opposing categories, impartial, unaffiliated

I am liberal, but my brother is conservative, so to avoid offending either of us my mother tries to be politically ***neutral.***

v. neutralize *n.* neutrality, neutralization *adj.* neutralized *adv.* neutrally

eliminating, eliminated, eliminated
to get rid of, to remove or exclude

First he became a vegetarian; now he is trying to ***eliminate*** *milk from his diet.*

n. elimination

NEUTRAL
adjective

INJURE

verb

exactly the same

We hoped the other airline would be cheaper, but the ticket prices were ***identical.***

adv. identically

injuring, injured, injured
to hurt

*She was badly **injured** in a skiing accident.*

n. injury *adj.* injurious, injured *adv.* injuriously

IDENTICAL
adjective

DEPLETE

verb

legally responsible

*Parents are **liable** for damage caused by their children.*

n. liability

depleting, depleted, depleted

to use up

*Some critics worry that we are rapidly **depleting** the world's oil supply.*

n. depletion

LIABLE

adjective

TRANSFORM

verb

strongest or most prevalent, foremost, main, primary

The cake is supposed to be chocolate mocha, but the ***predominant*** *flavor is coffee.*

v. predominate *n.* predominance *adv.* predominantly

transforming, transformed, transformed
to change dramatically

*The discovery of penicillin **transformed** the way doctors treat infections.*

n. transformation

PREDOMINANT

adjective

PERMIT

verb

hard to believe, amazing, remarkable

*He has an **incredible** ability to learn new languages quickly.*

adv. incredibly

permitting, permitted, permitted
to allow

The police refused to ***permit*** *the protest.*

n. permission, permit *adj.* permitted, permissive *adv.* permissively

INCREDIBLE
adjective

JUSTIFY

verb

resembling something else, alike

Oranges and tangerines are ***similar*** *fruits.*

n. similarity *adv.* similarly

justifying, justified, justified

to show or claim that (something) is right or reasonable

*He tried to **justify** his theft by claiming the money was owed to him.*

n. justification *adj.* justifiable, justified *adv.* justifiably

SIMILAR

adjective

FLUCTUATE

verb

consistent with logic and reason, reasonable, logical

A good judge must be ***rational,*** *and not easily swayed by emotion.*

v. rationalize *n.* rationality, rationalization, rationalist *adv.* rationally

fluctuating, fluctuated, fluctuated
to vary frequently and irregularly, to vacillate

The temperature has been ***fluctuating*** *a lot recently, so I wasn't sure if I should wear a coat.*

n. fluctuation *adj.* fluctuating

RATIONAL

adjective

DEVIATE

verb

without order or organization

The seating assignments were ***random.***

n. random, randomness *adv.* randomly

deviating, deviated, deviated
to differ or stray from an established standard or course, to vary or diverge

The final version of the building ***deviated*** *only slightly from the original plan.*

n. deviation, deviant *adj.* deviant

RANDOM
adjective

EXPORT
verb

basic, essential, intrinsic

*The Supreme Court has recognized that all citizens have a **fundamental** right to privacy.*

n. fundamental *adv.* fundamentally

exporting, exported, exported

to send something out of the country, usually for sale

*Their business **exports** dairy products to Europe.*

n. exporter, export, exporting *adj.* exported

FUNDAMENTAL

adjective

IMPORT

verb

short

*There will be a **brief** announcement before class today.*

n. brevity *adv.* briefly

importing, imported, imported
to bring something into the country, usually for sale

*He **imports** wine from Europe.*

n. importer, import, importing *adj.* imported

BRIEF

adjective

REGULATE

verb

shared by or affecting both parties

*My parents made a **mutual** decision to sell the house.*

adv. mutually

regulating, regulated, regulated
to control, especially by making rules, to supervise

*The government **regulates** the sale of certain medicines.*

n. regulation, regulator *adj.* regulatory, regulated

MUTUAL

adjective

PROVIDE
verb

easily seen or recognized; clear

*It was **obvious** that she was going to win.*

adv. obviously

providing, provided, provided
to supply

*The local bakery **provided** cakes for our bake sale.*

n. provision, provider

adjective

OBVIOUS

QUALIFY

verb

impossible to prevent, unavoidable

He was a dangerous driver, and it was ***inevitable*** *that he would eventually get into an accident.*

n. inevitability *adv.* inevitably

qualifying, qualified, qualified
to meet requirements, to be or become eligible

*By winning the game they **qualified** for the national tournament.*

n. qualification, qualifier *adj.* qualified, qualifying

INEVITABLE
adjective

SUCCEED

verb

unlikely to change or shift, secure

It is best for children to grow up in ***stable*** *homes.*

v. stabilize *n.* stability, stabilization *adv.* stably

succeeding, succeeded, succeeded
to achieve a goal

*He finally **succeeded** in getting his novel published.*

n. success *adj.* successful *adv.* successfully

STABLE

adjective

REMOVE

verb

opposite, contradictory, conflicting

No matter what I say, you always argue the ***contrary*** *position.*

n. contrary *adv.* contrarily

removing, removed, removed
to take (something) off or away

*You must **remove** the peel before eating a banana.*

n. removal *adj.* removable

CONTRARY
adjective

COMMIT

verb

characteristic, special, unique

Asparagus has a ***distinctive*** taste.

n. distinction *adj.* distinct *adv.* distinctively, distinctly

committing, committed, committed

1. to promise to do something, to pledge; 2. to carry out (a crime, etc.)

*We **committed** to working here until the end of the summer.*

*I never thought I could **commit** murder.*

n. commitment *adj.* committed

DISTINCTIVE

adjective

GENERATE
verb

prior
Do you have any ***previous*** *experience?*
adv. previously

generating, generated, generated
to produce, to create

*Her latest movie has **generated** a lot of controversy.*

PREVIOUS
adjective

allowed by or relating to the law, lawful

*Alcoholic beverages were banned in the United States from 1919 until 1933, when prohibition ended and they became **legal** again.*

v. legalize *n.* legalization, legality *adj.* legalized *adv.* legally

FOCUS

verb

focusing, focused, focused
to direct one's attention to, to concentrate

*We need to **focus** on the problem of water pollution before it is too late.*

n. focus *adj.* focused

LEGAL

adjective

IDENTIFY

verb

cultural, united or defined by culture, tradition, or nationality

The event was intended to promote understanding between members of different ***ethnic*** *groups.*

n. ethnicity *adv.* ethnically

identifying, identified, identified

to determine who or what a person or thing is, to recognize

*She **identified** him as the man who tried to sell her a stolen watch.*

n. identity, identification *adj.* identifiable, identified

ETHNIC

adjective

PERSUADE

verb

great in amount or extent, sizable, substantial, significant

The first European colonists in North America faced ***considerable*** *hardships during the cold winter months.*

adv. considerably

persuading, persuaded, persuaded

to convince

*I was planning to stay here over the vacation, but my parents **persuaded** me to come home instead.*

n. persuasion *adj.* persuasive *adv.* persuasively

CONSIDERABLE

adjective

ORGANIZE

verb

of the least possible amount or degree

They set a ***minimum*** *GPA of 3.5 for applicants to the honors program.*

v. minimize *n.* minimum, minimization *adj.* minimal *adv.* minimally

organizing, organized, organized

1. to put in order; 2. to arrange

*I must **organize** my desk so I can find things more easily.*

*They are **organizing** a concert to benefit local charities.*

n. organization, organizer *adj.* organized

MINIMUM

adjective

TOLERATE

verb

of the greatest possible amount or degree, most

I got a ticket for driving over the ***maximum*** *speed.*

v. maximize *n.* maximum, maximization *adj.* maximal *adv.* maximally

tolerating, tolerated, tolerated
to allow or endure

*My boss doesn't **tolerate** lateness.*

n. tolerance *adj.* tolerant, tolerable *adv.* tolerantly, tolerably

MAXIMUM
adjective

worthy of attention, important, remarkable

*There has been a **significant** increase in the annual number of forest fires.*

n. significance *adv.* significantly

GUARANTEE

verb

guaranteeing, guaranteed, guaranteed
to promise or ensure

*Can you **guarantee** that this program will work on my computer?*

n. guarantee *adj.* guaranteed

SIGNIFICANT
adjective

CONTRIBUTE

verb

lasting a short time

This won't work forever; it's only a ***temporary*** *solution.*

adv. temporarily

contributing, contributed, contributed
to give or donate

*All of the parents were asked to **contribute** twenty dollars for new soccer uniforms.*

n. contribution, contributor *adj.* contributed, contributing

TEMPORARY
adjective

COINCIDE

verb

unbiased; unprejudiced

*We need an **objective** judge to tell us whose singing is better.*

n. objectivity *adv.* objectively

coinciding, coincided, coincided
to happen at the same time

*Her visit **coincided** with the annual Folk Music Festival.*

n. coincidence *adj.* coincidental *adv.* coincidentally

OBJECTIVE
adjective

CONTRADICT

verb

complete, thorough

With this ***comprehensive*** *collection of recipes, you'll never need another cookbook.*

adv. comprehensively

contradicting, contradicted, contradicted
to oppose or challenge (a person or statement), to dispute

*He **contradicted** your version of the story.*

n. contradiction *adj.* contradictory

COMPREHENSIVE
adjective

RECOVER

verb

necessary in order for something to be complete, extremely important

*You are an **integral** part of this project; we couldn't do it without you.*

adv. integrally

recovering, recovered, recovered
to improve after experiencing a decline

The economy ***recovered*** *quickly after the recent recession.*

n. recovery *adj.* recoverable

INTEGRAL

adjective

PERPETUATE

verb

natural, consistent with what is expected

*Is it **normal** for a baby to walk so early?*

v. normalize *n.* normality, normalization *adj.* normalized *adv.* normally

perpetuating, perpetuated, perpetuated
to cause (something) to last indefinitely, to sustain

Advertisements like these ***perpetuate*** *sexism in our society.*

n. perpetuity *adj.* perpetual *adv.* perpetually

NORMAL
adjective

EXCLUDE

verb

able to do something, competent

Many scientists still doubt that apes are ***capable*** *of using complex language.*

n. capability

excluding, excluded, excluded
to leave out, to omit

*The boys were **excluded** from the game.*

n. exclusion *adj.* exclusionary, exclusive, excluded *adv.* exclusively

CAPABLE

adjective

ESTIMATE

verb

readily obtained, possible to get

*This chair is **available** in six different colors.*

n. availability

estimating, estimated, estimated
to make an educated guess

*We **estimate** that next year's profits will be 20 percent higher.*

n. estimate, estimation *adj.* estimated

AVAILABLE

adjective

LEGISLATE

verb

safe, assured

Make sure to keep your valuables in a ***secure*** *place.*

v. secure *n.* security *adv.* securely

legislating, legislated, legislated
to make law

*Congress **legislated** a federal minimum wage in 1938.*

n. legislation, legislator, legislature *adj.* legislative *adv.* legislatively

SECURE
adjective

INDICATE

verb

exceptional, special, one of a kind

Her style is ***unique****.*

n. uniqueness *adv.* uniquely

indicating, indicated, indicated
to show or suggest

*Your test scores **indicate** exceptional talent in math.*

n. indication, indicator *adj.* indicative

UNIQUE
adjective

endless, limitless, innumerable, so great as to be impossible to measure or count

The universe is so immensely large that many consider it to be ***infinite.***

n. infinity *adv.* infinitely

EDIT

verb

editing, edited, edited
to change and improve a piece of writing

Your manuscript is strong, but it needs to be ***edited.***

n. editor, edition *adj.* editorial *adv.* editorially

INFINITE

adjective

STRAIGHTFORWARD

adjective

good, having a positive effect

Vitamin A is said to be ***beneficial*** *for the eyes.*

n. benefit *adv.* beneficially

uncomplicated, simple

*An effective speech will be **straightforward** and have a clear point.*

n. straightforwardness *adv.* straightforwardly

BENEFICIAL

adjective

PRELIMINARY

adjective

noteworthy, striking, extraordinary

Since the new program began, there has been a **remarkable** *increase in the number of applicants to the school.*

adv. remarkably

coming before or done in preparation for something

Before starting the program, you will need to take a ***preliminary*** *course.*

n. preliminary

REMARKABLE

adjective

VALUABLE

adjective

preexisting, earlier

*Most students in the class have some **prior** knowledge of the subject.*

of great worth, expensive

*The discs contained very **valuable** information.*

v. value *n.* value *adj.* valued

PRIOR

adjective

RELUCTANT

adjective

connected to what is being considered, pertinent, applicable

The judge ruled that this information wasn't ***relevant*** to the case.

n. relevance *adv.* relevantly

unwilling; not eager

*She got the scholarship, but she is **reluctant** to move abroad.*

n. reluctance *adv.* reluctantly

RELEVANT

adjective

concerning or consistent with accepted moral standards, moral

Doctors disagree about whether it is ***ethical*** *to transplant kidneys from living donors.*

n. ethic *adv.* ethically

SUBTLE

adjective

delicate or understated, not obvious

Though garlic can be overpowering, in this recipe it is quite ***subtle****.*

n. subtletly *adv.* subtly

ETHICAL

adjective

VAGUE

adjective

relating to the mind, intellectual or psychological

Her strange behavior led doctors to suspect she was suffering from a ***mental*** *illness.*

n. mentality *adv.* mentally

unclear, imprecise; not specific

I don't remember exactly what he looked like, but I have a ***vague*** *memory.*

n. vagueness *adv.* vaguely

MENTAL

adjective

CONSISTENT

adjective

solitary, alone

The cabin was completely ***isolated*** *in the middle of the forest.*

v. isolate *n.* isolation, isolationism

1. unchanging, stable; 2. compatible, in line with

*To train your dog you must be **consistent** about disciplining him.*

*The results of the blood test were **consistent** with the diagnosis.*

n. consistency *adv.* consistently

ISOLATED

adjective

EQUIVALENT
adjective

occurring once each year; yearly
*I'm taking my car to the mechanic for its **annual** inspection.*
adv. annually

equal

*One gallon is **equivalent** to four quarts.*

n. equivalent, equivalence, equivalency *adv.* equivalently

ANNUAL

adjective

VALID
adjective

fully grown; aged; adult
He has become much more ***mature*** *since he went away to college.*
v. mature *n.* maturity, maturation

1. acceptable as true; reasonable, convincing; 2. legally binding or effective; legitimate

*She made a very **valid** point about the risks of this investment.*

*He will leave the country soon, because his visa is only **valid** until next week.*

v. validate *n.* validity, validation *adj.* validated *adv.* validly

MATURE

adjective

WIDESPREAD
adjective

nervous, worried that something bad will happen
He is ***apprehensive*** *about the interview.*
n. apprehensiveness *adv.* apprehensively

affecting or existing in a large area; extensive; general

*The storm caused **widespread** damage, with flooding in six states.*

APPREHENSIVE

adjective

RIGID
adjective

main, major, most important or significant
Taxes were one of the ***primary*** *reasons that the American colonies declared independence.*
n. primacy *adj.* prime *adv.* primarily

hard, stiff, unyielding

*There is a **rigid** dress code at his new school that forbids jeans and sneakers.*

n. rigidity *adv.* rigidly

PRIMARY

adjective

1. acquainted, having knowledge of; 2. well-known, friendly

*I've read many of his books, so I'm **familiar** with his theories.*

*It was good to see a **familiar** face after my long stay abroad.*

n. familiarity

ULTIMATE

adjective

1. eventual, final; 2. ideal, best

Her musical career started badly, but her talent and dedication ensured ***ultimate*** *success.*

This is the ***ultimate*** *chocolate brownie: rich and chewy.*

n. ultimate, ultimatum *adv.* ultimately

FAMILIAR

adjective

ABSTRACT

adjective

that which operates or happens on its own, self-activating

The lights are on an ***automatic*** *timer, so they turn on every night even if no one is home.*

v. automate *n.* automation *adj.* automated *adv.* automatically

based on ideas or general concepts rather than physical reality or specific events

This aspect of economics seems very ***abstract,*** *but it has important real-life applications.*

n. abstraction, abstract *adv.* abstractly

AUTOMATIC

adjective

IGNORANT

adjective

relating to health care and the science of treating diseases

*My son wants to get a **medical** degree and become a doctor or nurse.*

v. medicate *n.* medicine *adv.* medically

lacking in knowledge, unaware, uneducated

*He knows a lot about most sports, but when it comes to hockey he is completely **ignorant**.*

n. ignorance, ignoramus *adv.* ignorantly

MEDICAL

adjective

EXTENSIVE

adjective

---

suitable for; able to work with

His style of acting was more ***compatible*** *with film than with television.*

n. compatibility

wide-reaching, broad, substantial

*She has **extensive** experience with a variety of computer systems.*

v. extend *n.* extent *adv.* extensively

COMPATIBLE

adjective

UNIVERSAL

adjective

able to be interpreted in more than one way, unclear

*We had a long debate over some **ambiguous** passages in Hamlet.*

n. ambiguity, ambiguousness *adv.* ambiguously

applying to all people or situations

*Fear of the unknown is a **universal** human trait.*

n. universality *adv.* universally

AMBIGUOUS

adjective

POSITIVE

adjective

extreme, severe

People with appendicitis experience ***intense*** *abdominal pain.*

v. intensify *n.* intensity, intensification *adj.* intensive, intensified *adv.* intensely, intensively

good, not negative

*The new rules should have a **positive** effect on safety.*

adv. positively

INTENSE

adjective

VISIBLE

adjective

extremely small; minute; tiny

The water is safe to drink, but it has a ***miniscule*** *amount of contamination.*

able to be seen

*The fish were **visible** through the clear water.*

n. visibility *adv.* visibly

MINUSCULE

adjective

ESSENTIAL

adjective

intelligent, relating to intelligence, academic, educated

She reads a lot, and our conversations are usually very ***intellectual.***

n. intellect, intellectual *adv.* intellectually

absolutely necessary, crucial

*Good water is **essential** for making good tea.*

n. essence *adv.* essentially

INTELLECTUAL

adjective

ENORMOUS

adjective

enough

The oxygen in the tank is ***sufficient*** *for a one-hour dive.*

v. suffice *n.* sufficiency *adv.* sufficiently

immensely large; huge

The fossil is an ***enormous*** *footprint that may have been made by a dinosaur.*

n. enormity *adv.* enormously

SUFFICIENT

adjective

DOMESTIC

adjective

fast, quick

The ambulance crew has to provide a ***rapid*** *response in emergencies.*

n. rapidity *adv.* rapidly

1. relating to the home or housework; 2. existing, originating or taking place within a particular country

Women and men today are likely to share the burden of ***domestic*** *tasks.*

Voters tend to be more interested in ***domestic*** *issues than in foreign affairs.*

n. domesticity, domestic *adv.* domestically

RAPID

adjective

of as much quantity or quality as is needed, sufficient, enough

The climbers left base camp with ***adequate*** *supplies for a three-day journey.*

n. adequacy *adv.* adequately

FINAL

adjective

last

Tomorrow is the ***final*** *day of classes for the fall semester.*

v. finalize *n.* finality, finalization, final *adv.* finally

ADEQUATE

adjective

ACCURATE
adjective

able to be thought of, imaginable

*We used every **conceivable** method to raise money for the project.*

v. conceive *adv.* conceivably

perfectly correct, without errors

He always checks his bill before paying to make sure it is ***accurate.***

n. accuracy *adv.* accurately

CONCEIVABLE

adjective